Chocola Island

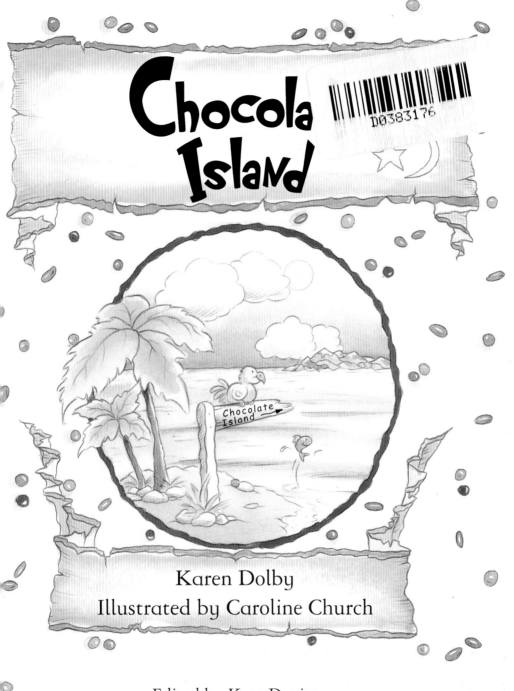

Karen Dolby

Illustrated by Caroline Church

Edited by Kate Davies
Cover design by Will Dawes

Contents

3 How it all started
4 The chocolate cake competition
6 Granny Truffle's story
8 The old map
11 Aboard the *Chocolate Queen*
12 Chocolate Island
14 The Chocolate Chip Mine
16 Chocolate Falls
18 Inside the Cookie Café
20 The Chocolate Signpost
22 Syrup Swamp
24 Mallow Maze
26 The Chocolate Well
28 Competition time
30 The winner's cup
31 Answers

How it all started

Tom and Grace are really excited. They've just spotted a poster for an amazing baking contest...

Chunkies Chocolate Cakes and Cookies Competition

to bake the best ever Chocolate Cake

Sensational prizes:
World fame as a cook. Television appearances. Lifetime's supply of chocolate cakes and cookies.

his book is full of puzzles to solve.

If you get stuck, there are answers on pages 31 and 32.

The chocolate cake competition

Tom and Grace jumped up and down with excitement when they saw the poster. "Let's go and tell Uncle Ollie!" said Grace, breathlessly.

"He bakes the yummiest chocolate cakes in the world. I'm sure he can win!"

They raced to Uncle Ollie's house, and waved the leaflet at him. "Read this, Uncle Ollie!" panted Tom.

"I can't see a thing without my spectacles," said Uncle Ollie.

Can you find Ollie's spectacles?

Granny Truffle's story

Uncle Ollie sighed. "We won't beat Mrs. Nougat. Her chocolate cake is famous."

Tom pulled a face. "But she's so mean!"

"My Granny Truffle made the most stunningly chocolatey cake in the world," said Ollie. "We'd win if I could find her recipe – and chocolate from the Chocolate Island Well. She used to tell me about it when I was a boy."

"A well full of chocolate? A Chocolate Island? It can't be true!" said Grace and Tom.

"But it is!" exclaimed Uncle Ollie. "Imagine a place where chocolate grows on trees and fudge flows in the streams... I have a map of it somewhere. It has the Chocolate Island symbol of a moon and a star on it."

Can you see the Chocolate Island map?

The old map

Grace picked up the old map.
"We have to visit Chocolate
Island!" cried Tom, excitedly.

OLLIE'S
HOUSE

CHOCOLATE
ISLAND
FERRY

Grace agreed. "Uncle Ollie's baking the cake, so it's up to us to bring him the chocolate."

Which is Chocolate Island?

CHOCOLATE
QUEEN

Aboard the Chocolate Queen

They dashed to the seashore and found a strange boat waiting. "Hold on tight, me hearties!" cried Captain Cook, as the boat shot into the air.

"We're flying!" gasped Grace, gazing down into the sparkling sea.

It wasn't long before Tom spotted Chocolate Island. He recognized the fudge stream, chocolate drop trees and chocolate pebbles on the beach.

Can you find all the things Tom saw?

Chocolate Island

When they landed, Captain Cook gave Grace a purse. "It's full of Chocolate Island pennies," she said. "Watch out for the golden gloop, and don't trust the whistling candy trees..."

Hello! I'm a Chocolate Island guide.

Grace and Tom licked their lips as the guide showed them around.

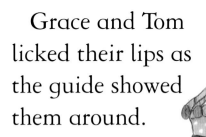

This is Hansel and Gretel's house. The gingerbread walls are delicious!

"Tiggy will help you find the Chocolate Well," she said. "He's under the tree with white flowers growing on it."

Can you see Tiggy?

The Chocolate Chip Mine

Under the tree lay Tiggy, a sleepy tiger.

"You're looking for the Chocolate Well,"
he yawned. "You must visit the
Chocolate Chip Mine and the
waterfalls first," he said.
"They're spectacular!"

He led them to a
cable car at the top
of the mine.

Tom and Grace stepped out of the cable car and gazed at the towering caverns. There were miners on all sides, chipping away at the chocolate in the rocks.

How many miners are there?

Chocolate Falls

They left the mine and headed for the waterfalls, which were bubbling over rocks into a shimmering rainbow pool.

"It looks like chocolate milkshake," said Grace, as Tom dived in.

Grace jumped in after Tom, and soon they were happily splashing around in the chocolate. Then, an enormous spotted toad appeared by the pool. It waved them over, and started croaking out a message.

What is the toad's message?

Inside the Cookie Café

When Tom and Grace entered the café, they were greeted by smiling faces and the delicious smell of baking. Everyone wanted to help them find the well.

Buy your copy of Granny Truffle's Recipe Book HERE 12 CI Pennies

Granny Truffle

Follow the crispy crackle path to the signpost.

Just as they were about to leave, Grace spotted something. "Uncle Ollie will find that useful. Lucky we have that purse full of Chocolate Island pennies!"

What has Grace found?

The Chocolate Signpost

Grace and Tom left the café, and set off along the crispy crackle path. "It's made of crunchy chocolate!" exclaimed Grace, stopping to break off a piece.

"Hurry up!" called Tom, crossing the bridge over the Bubbling Brook. "We have to find the signpost."

When they found the Chocolate Signpost, it was hard to read. A chubby squirrel had bitten off lots of pieces. Tom picked up a broken piece which said "Tower".

"If we can match this to the signpost, we'll know which path leads to Toffee Tower."

Which path should they take?

Syrup Swamp

They set off for Toffee Tower. Soon, Tom found it hard to lift his feet. He was squelching through sticky syrup. Suddenly he started sinking, deeper and deeper every second. "Help!" he yelled.

Then, the candy trees began to sway. They whistled and whispered to Tom.

"Step on the golden gloop stones and avoid the ghastly green ones," the trees hissed. But Grace wasn't so sure.

"Wait!" she shouted. "Remember what Captain Cook told us when we arrived?"

What do you think Tom should do?

Mallow Maze

At last, they reached the tower.

"I'll race you to the top," called Grace, running ahead. "We can look down from that balcony and plan our route through the maze."

"I can't wait till we reach the Chocolate Well!" yelled Tom.

Can you find a path through the maze to the well?

The Chocolate Well

When they reached the well, they pulled up the bucket and dipped their fingers into the chocolate. It was the smoothest, creamiest, most magical chocolate in the world.

But time was running out. They had to get home quickly, so that Uncle Ollie could bake his cake in time for the competition.

They raced to the beach, but the ferry had gone. Just then, a familiar face appeared.

There's an underwater path which is safe to cross when the water is less than knee deep.

Is it safe to cross the underwater path?

If there is no ferry you may be able to cross by the underwater path
The water is over your head depth at 8 o'clock
It's shoulder deep at 10 o'clock
Knee deep at 12 o'clock
Ankle deep at 2 o'clock
Toe deep at 4 o'clock

Competition time

Grace and Tom splashed through the path, and rushed back to Uncle Ollie's house.

Ollie mixed the ingredients for Granny Truffle's sensational chocolate cake recipe. Last of all he added the magical Chocolate Island chocolate.

The finished cake looked and smelled delicious. At the competition, the judges seemed impressed. They even came back for second helpings. But someone wasn't happy about the way the contest was going...

Can you see who it is?
Which do you think is Uncle Ollie's cake?

29

The winner's cup

There was silence as the chief judge began to speak. "There was one chocolate cake which was simply magical," he said. "The winner is... Ollie!"

Everyone cheered as Uncle Ollie held up the winner's cup above his head. Tom and Grace jumped up and down with joy.

"Hooray for Chocolate Island!" they cried, "and the best ever adventure!"

Answers

Pages 4-5
Uncle Ollie's spectacles are here.

Pages 6-7
The map is circled here. You can see the moon and star sign in the corner.

Pages 8-9
Chocolate Island is here.

You can see the Chocolate Island symbol of the moon and star on the signpost.

Pages 10-11
This is Chocolate Island.

You can see the chocolate fudge stream and chocolate drop trees marked here.

Pages 12-13
You can see Tiggy here under the tree.

Pages 14-15
There are eleven chocolate chip miners. You can see them all circled here.

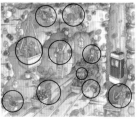

Pages 16-17
The message is:
GO TO THE
COOKIE CAFÉ.

Pages 18-19

Grace has spotted a sign for Granny Truffle's Chocolate Recipe Book. They can use the Chocolate Island pennies that Captain Cook gave them to buy a copy.

Pages 20-21

The broken piece which says "Tower" matches this part of the signpost. Grace and Tom must take this path to the Toffee Tower.

Pages 22-23

Captain Cook told them to: "Watch out for the golden gloop, and don't trust the whistling candy trees." (See page 12.) Grace knows that Tom should not do what the trees are telling him. To cross the syrup swap he must only walk on the green stones and avoid the golden stones.

Pages 24-25

The route through the maze is marked here in blue.

Pages 26-27

The clock on the Toffee Tower shows the time is 2:30 and the signpost tells them the water is less than ankle deep at that time. This means it is safe for Grace and Tom to cross the underwater path back to the mainland and home.

Pages 28-29

Mrs. Nougat is not very happy. You can recognize her from page 6. Ollie's cake has the Chocolate Island moon and star sign as decoration.

Mrs. Nougat

Ollie's cake

By the way . . . did you spot Captain Cook appearing throughout the story? You can see her on page 4 at the shop window; on pages 10 and 12 with her boat; helping Tom and Grace on page 27; and as one of the judges on page 29.

This edition first published in 2007 by Usborne Publishing Ltd., Usborne House, 83-85 Saffron Hill, London EC1N 8RT, England. www.usborne.com Copyright © 2007, 2002, 1995 Usborne Publishing Ltd. The name Usborne and the devices ⊕ are Trade Marks of Usborne Publishing Ltd. All rights reserved.